AF690013

Money

Good and Bad

Roy A. Minet

While every precaution has been taken in the preparation of this book, the publisher assumes no responsibility for errors or omissions, or for damages resulting from the use of the information contained herein.

Money

Good and Bad

First Edition. June 6, 2025.

Copyright © 2025 Roy A. Minet.

Written by Roy A. Minet.

0. Preface

Do **you** understand money? Should you buy some Bitcoin? How about gold? Silver? What causes inflation and can it be prevented? How? Can you explain the three functions that money needs to perform well? What are the three basic kinds of money and which of the kinds is cryptocurrency?

Everyone deals with money on a daily basis. Few give it much thought. But if you're a bit fuzzy about the answers to any of the above questions, it could be hazardous to your wealth. There have been many problems with money, some of them quite disruptive. Sound money is very important to the proper functioning of a free market economy.

This short, easy-to-read book aims to clarify some confusing aspects of money. It will provide the knowledge to answer the above questions and many more. For their own good, citizens and informed voters need to be able to evaluate the validity of politician's proposals and government policies regarding money. As a bonus, the ultimate sound currency is proposed.

Table of Contents

1. The Origins of Money

Many millennia ago, there was very little of anything that could be called economic activity among people. That is, individuals and families were pretty much isolated economic entities that had to produce for themselves substantially everything they needed: food, shelter, clothing, and so on. Just surviving was more than a full-time job; the less fit were unable to support themselves and perished or became food for wild animals. There was no need for money.

Over time, people learned that they could be more successful (achieve a higher standard of living) through peaceful cooperation. To facilitate cooperation, they began banding together in communities. It's hard to be peaceful if everybody is stealing everybody else's stuff, so maintaining peace required respect for the ownership of *private property*.

About twelve millennia ago, the advent of agriculture catalyzed a major shift away from nomadic hunting and gathering and toward more permanent farming settlements. It was then realized that some people were much better hunters than others, while other people were better at farming, building shelters, making clothes, or other tasks. Much higher overall productivity could be obtained through *specialization*. Not only could each person spend most of their time doing what they were best at doing, but they could also further hone their skills and knowledge as well as justify making specialized tools to further boost productivity.

With specialization came the need to exchange commodities. Suppose you specialized in farming. Presumably, you would have lots of food available to you, more than you could consume yourself. But you would lack all the other things you need. You would have to trade some of your excess food with other specialists for the things you need that they have produced. When you needed a new pair of shoes, you would reach an agreement with a cobbler to trade some food for a pair of shoes. Of course, the same applied to everyone else who would need to trade some of what they had produced for food.

Each such transaction is called a *voluntary exchange*. Many such trades form a barter economy where various types of goods or services are swapped for all manner of other goods or services. Now, instead of each individual or family being an isolated economic entity, there were many people interacting among each other through what is called an economy.

A barter economy surely works, but the exchanges tend to be a bit clumsy and inconvenient. Money might help.

The Three Functions of Money

In order to best facilitate exchanges, there are three functions money needs to perform well. They are:

1. **Provide a convenient medium of exchange:** Money needs to be available whenever and wherever it is needed. In the past, that meant it was easy to carry around in any reasonable amount, but technology is now in the process of obviating that requirement. Money needs to be divisible to a fine enough level that amounts that exactly match the

value of any transaction can be easily transferred. Money should be durable and difficult to duplicate or counterfeit. It would also be nice if money were difficult to steal.

2. **Act as a standard of value:** Just as a meterstick (or a yardstick) measures distance, money should establish a measure of value. It provides an easy way to compare the values of disparate things, such as bushels of corn, pairs of shoes, houses, and cows. The scale on a meterstick is fixed and enables distances to be measured reproducibly and accurately at different places and at different times. Just as stretchy rubber would not make a good meterstick, something with a varying value calibration does not make good money. A standard that changes cannot be a good standard. Having a good measure of value enables financial tracking, calculations, and projections.

3. **Provide a mechanism to store value:** As a farmer, you harvest your corn in the fall, but you may not need a new pair of shoes at that time. Money enables you to sell your

corn when you harvest it, store its value as money, and buy shoes (as well as other things) later whenever you need them. Thus, the use of money decouples the two ends of a transaction and enables them to happen at different times and places. Money also facilitates saving and lending. Obviously, money's ability to store value is seriously impaired to the degree that money does not act as a good standard of value.

Money that performs all three of these functions well — especially functions 2 and 3 — is known as *sound money, good money*, or a *hard currency*. When more than one form of money is circulating, people prefer to hang onto and accumulate (or save) the sound money and get rid of (spend) the bad money. This natural, logical, and easily understandable phenomenon is known as Gresham's Law. If the bad money is bad enough, it loses value and eventually falls into disuse.

The First Money

People have tried to use a wide variety of physical things as money. Early attempts were prehistoric, therefore, unknown. It appears that various weights of barley may have been about the first thing to be widely used as money over a substantial period of time, but silver coins also appeared quite early. The *shekel* was a unit of weight (about 10 grams or a third of an ounce) and small silver coins of that weight were a very early currency. Other things were valued in terms of shekels or fractions of a shekel.

Later, but still several hundred years BCE, both gold and silver coins came into more widespread use and have demonstrated considerable staying power ever since. Different weights of precious metals perform the above three functions of money quite well, and they are still used today. These types of money are called ***commodity money*** because a designated commodity that itself has intrinsic value is used as money.

For improved convenience, ***representative money*** eventually came into use. A commodity (e.g., gold or silver) was deposited with a dealer or a bank for safekeeping. Receipts were issued for which the commodity could later be reclaimed or withdrawn. The receipts, frequently called *bank notes*, were used as currency (primarily for larger amounts) in parallel with circulating coins to handle smaller amounts. Although the receipts or bank notes themselves had little or no intrinsic value, any holder was guaranteed to be able to convert them to something that did have value at any time upon the request of the bearer. It was far easier to carry bank notes around than large amounts of heavy precious metals.

The immutable laws of economics dictate that the value of any and every commodity in an economy is always set by the availability (supply) of the commodity relative to the demand for it. There have been many foolish attempts to force the value (price) of various commodities to some desired amount, but those who attempt to defeat the laws of economics inevitably lose.

Of course, it is possible that the supply and/or demand for a commodity (therefore its price), especially one traded in small volumes, could be manipulated. Someone could offer for sale large amounts of a commodity at an artificially low price or buy large amounts at an artificially high price. Obviously, either would be to the disadvantage of the manipulator and could not long continue before the manipulator's resources were depleted. Scurrilous promulgation of misinformation, either to increase or decrease demand, might be more cost-effective, but such lies become evident fairly quickly. Thus, any manipulation, if successful at all, is bound to be short-lived, so any advantage to be reaped from manipulation needs to be nailed down quickly.

However, since the supply of and demand for anything can validly change over time, it is entirely possible, even probable, that the value of any given commodity *will* change over time. Thus, commodity money has the disadvantage that the value of everything is measured relative to the value of the chosen commodity, which is not always constant. To the degree that a commodity's value relative to other commodities is not constant, that commodity's ability to act as a standard of value and a store of value is necessarily impaired.

Gold has performed the three functions of money fairly well over a remarkably long period of time. An important reason for this is that gold is durable and its supply is fairly inelastic. More gold cannot be created without significant cost and effort. Another reason is that despite some short-term fluctuation, the value of gold relative to everything else has remained surprisingly constant over the long term. Of course, there is no guarantee that this will always continue to be true in the future.

Commodity money does have one very big advantage: it has a substantial intrinsic value that is never zero. Representative money also has this advantage, although there is some added risk that the dealer or other depository may not actually still have the commodity that was supposed to be in safekeeping when someone shows up to reclaim it.

Fiat Currency

Soon after the end of the first millennium CE, the "innovation" of ***fiat money*** burst onto the scene. Like representative money, fiat money consists of bills or tokens that have substantially zero intrinsic value (or the intrinsic value is far below the face value). But unlike representative money, fiat money does not represent anything at all. There is no guarantee that it can be redeemed for any amount of anything of value. Its value is simply decreed by law or fiat.

Suppose you made up some paper bills in your basement with a "1" or "One" and a nice headshot of yourself printed on them. You then declare that each of your bills is worth one ounce of silver. Now you boogie on down to the store and exchange some of your fiat bills for groceries and clothing. That is all there is to a fiat currency. The only difference is that it is normally a government that prints the currency and decrees its value, not an individual. Unless the individual happens to be the dictator of record, they will not be able to use force to back up their decree or fiat.

The first fiat currency was attempted approximately a thousand years ago by the Song Dynasty in China. Paper bills were issued and decreed to be exchangeable for certain amounts of gold, silver, or silk. However, no way was provided to actually redeem the bills for these commodities or anything else of intrinsic value. This realization, combined with the printing of many bills, caused people to lose confidence in the currency. The government attempted to force the use of the currency by insisting that taxes be partially paid with the bills, but nevertheless, rampant inflation (loss of perceived and functional value) completely killed the currency.

In view of the abject failure of the first fiat currency, no one would try that again, right? Wrong. Many fiat currencies have been attempted, and many have failed when the currency collapsed to its true value: zero. Considering its nature, it is not at all surprising that there have been, and continue to be, so many fiat currency failures. What is shocking is that there actually are examples of fiat currencies that have been made to work somewhat well for periods of several decades. How could something like that ever be pulled off?

In a totalitarian society, extreme oppressive force works pretty well. But even there, barter, black markets, and the use of precious metal coins still creep in "under the table" when people have little or no confidence in a fiat currency.

In freer societies, one fairly effective trick is to start out with a sound currency that is actually redeemable for something of real value—that is, a representative currency. Then, in the face of some "emergency," currency redeemability is "temporarily suspended." It works best if redeemability is suspended and restored a few times before "temporarily" suspending it permanently. People have by then been conditioned to continue to think their money is "as good as gold" since its redeemability is to be restored. Someday. Maybe.

If nothing disruptive occurs for a period of time following the last suspension of redemption "privileges," the "currency levitation" becomes self-perpetuating. It appears that a period of just a few decades without serious problems is all it takes to lull most people into a profound state of ignorance and complacency regarding their money.

In the final analysis, a person is willing to swap something of real value for a worthless piece of paper today if and only if they have confidence that they can swap the paper for something of reasonably equal value tomorrow. This is always, **always** true.

When a currency has been in use successfully for an extended period, people become more confident that it will continue to happen in the future. However, if and when this confidence is shaken, the collapse of a fiat currency is usually rapid and highly disruptive. The image comes to mind of the cartoon character that runs off a cliff but doesn't fall. After a suitable comedic interval, he looks down, realizes that absolutely nothing is holding him up, and then quickly crashes to the hard earth below.

2. Comparing the Three Kinds of Money

The first thing to note is that fiat money is created by force—an edict or fiat. On the other hand, commodity money and representative money come into use voluntarily among free and peaceful people. A fiat currency is monopolistic and entirely controlled by a government entity. Commodity money is the antithesis of this as it cannot be monopolistically controlled. Through the expenditure of work and effort, anyone can mine, grow, or otherwise create more of the commodity, but it cannot be created without limit for next-to-no cost.

Fiat money is political. If you move out of one political entity into another, you must change to using the fiat money demanded by the new political entity. Commodity money has intrinsic value and, therefore, can transcend political boundaries. Your gold coin will have substantially the same value (relative to other things) in any country, no matter whose likeness may have been stamped onto it.

Commodity money came into use and has been successfully used for thousands of years. Fiat money has been around for about the last thousand years. Fiat currencies tend not to last. There are a few examples where fiat currencies have been abandoned and phased out by the political entity that created it, but most have collapsed when people have lost confidence and reverted to using commodity money and/or barter.

One characteristic that affects a currency's ability to perform the functions of money well is the *elasticity* of its supply. The supply of substantially any commodity money tends to be quite inelastic. There is a definite cost to creating more of any commodity, and that turns out to be a good thing when it is used as money. Fiat money, with substantially zero intrinsic value, is almost completely elastic. Governments or skilled counterfeiters can create additional fiat money at near-zero cost essentially without limit.

Any sound money begins with something of value. You can exchange that thing for other things of value or for representative tokens (physical or electronic) with the guarantee that tokens can always be redeemed for something of equal value. A fiat currency starts instead with worthless tokens and attempts to force or bamboozle people to value them.

Inflation

With representative or commodity money, the value of everything is measured in terms of, or relative to, the chosen commodity (frequently gold), and the value of the currency is anchored to the value of that commodity. In order to issue more representative tokens of zero intrinsic value, it is necessary to hold more of the backing commodity "on deposit" since it is guaranteed that each token can be redeemed on demand for a certain fixed amount of the commodity. The value of such tokens is fixed and cannot float around. However, as previously noted, the value scale can change (either expand or contract) to the extent that the supply and/or demand of the backing commodity shifts and affects its value relative to everything else. This is the fundamental disadvantage of commodity or representative money that is based on a specific commodity.

Suppose you live in a country where the government has issued a representative currency based on gold. Said government holds the gold that backs the currency and "guarantees" that you can convert your dollars to gold on demand at the rate of $35 per ounce of gold. One morning, you learn through the news that the government has changed the exchange rate to $70 per ounce of gold, effective midnight of last night.

Surprise! Any money you had under your mattress or in the bank can now be redeemed for only half as much gold, and you will find that the prices of everything else in the stores will very quickly rise to approximately double as well. The currency has been devalued. That's a form of inflation. Although governments have done things this bad and worse, the change is normally carried out more gradually (in small steps spread out over time) to reduce economic disruption and avoid waking people up. Most people gripe about the prices going up instead of fingering the real culprit: the decreasing purchasing power of their money.

Of course, the government could decide to change the exchange rate in the other direction, say, to $20 per ounce of gold. That would be *de*flation. Don't hold your breath; this is not going to happen, as it would require the government to suddenly hold more gold to back the currency. By contrast, inflation enables the government to (elastically) print more worthless tokens backed by the same amount of gold.

Suppose now that you live in a country that has a fiat currency that has been successfully used for a few decades. What determines its value? Originally, the value was likely set when it was a hard currency convertible to something of real value. When this tie is removed (redeemability suspended), the value of the dollar (or other token) is no longer anchored to anything and begins to "float." Since it is not tied to anything, it becomes its own pseudo-commodity whose value depends upon its supply relative to its demand.

The supply is closely related to the total number of dollars in circulation, called the money supply. The demand is entirely determined by psychology! That is, people will value the dollar today based solely on how much value they expect they will be able to trade it for tomorrow or next week or next year, and the demand will be set by this consensus. Anything based on human expectations is affected by a huge complexity of factors and can potentially be quite volatile.

Increasing the money supply tends to reduce the value of the dollar, and vice versa, exactly as would be expected. When people have more dollars, they tend to bid up prices, and prices generally rise. The value of the dollar is reduced. This is inflation. Politicians and governments love to increase the money supply, so inflation is the rule, and deflation is a rare exception. Neither is good.

A simple demonstration, sometimes employed in the economics classroom, starkly illuminates the inflation process. The teacher produces and demonstrates the operation of a pocket flashlight that is no longer needed. It will be auctioned off to the highest bidder. Not being allowed to take students' "real" money, the teacher distributes $15 of monopoly money to each student to use in bidding. Students may combine resources if they are willing to jointly own or share the flashlight. The auction is conducted, and the flashlight sells for (typically) $25. Note that the worthless monopoly money has taken on a value only because the teacher is willing to exchange something of real value for it.

The teacher then produces and demonstrates a second identical flashlight, explaining that this is the only one remaining and that it, too, will be auctioned as before. An additional $15 is distributed to each student and the second auction conducted. The second flashlight typically sells for somewhere near $50. Quite obviously, the identical flashlight does not have a value greater than the first. The price has just gone up because the money supply has increased. More correctly, the value of each monopoly money dollar has decreased. The total value of all the worthless tokens in circulation tends to be proportional to the total value of the goods and services for which they can be traded.

Inflation (or deflation) seriously interferes with money's ability to act as a standard of value and, therefore, degrades its ability to act as a store of value. Some of the direct effects of inflation are that it:

- acts as a stealth tax as it quietly siphons wealth right out of wallets and bank accounts;
- discourages savings and accumulation of capital;
- pushes up interest rates;
- favors borrowers and hurts lenders (unless the loan interest rates are variable);
- interferes with the ability of businesses and individuals to plan for the future; and
- diminishes confidence in the currency.

Inflation pushes up interest rates because, if you want to charge 2% per year to rent out your money, you will need to collect 2% *plus* the expected rate of inflation. With 4% inflation the loan will be paid back with money that is worth 4% less each year, so you will have to collect 6% interest. Furthermore, after inflation gets going, the expectation of it continuing (or worse, the expectation that the rate of inflation will increase) tends to make it self-perpetuating and hard to bring under control.

A few macroeconomists have suggested that "moderate" rates of inflation have indirect effects that can be good, such as reducing unemployment. But these claims rest on complex and unproven macroeconomic theories. Fiat currencies and the inflation that they enable are, overall, not good for anybody. In fact, it is rapid inflation that usually triggers the collapse of a fiat currency. Inflation exceeding 25% to 40% annually is probably about the tipping point that leads to a degenerative inflationary spiral from which the currency does not recover. This has happened many times in many countries since the advent of fiat currencies.

Modern Developments

The advent of pervasive high-speed electronic communication and computation has had a significant impact. Transactions take place instantaneously at light speed. Accurate and detailed records are maintained by computers. The Internet has made rather complete information about virtually anything quickly and easily available. These capabilities have reduced market friction, a plethora of operational overhead costs, and enabled markets to operate more efficiently. In fact, numbers stored by computers have, to a considerable extent, replaced physical dollars in circulation. The money supply can be manipulated by changing numbers in computers.

Banks increase the money supply when they loan out the money that has been deposited into bank accounts by depositors. This is called *fractional reserve banking*. They hold enough cash in reserve to cover expected withdrawals plus some safety reserve. However, if too many depositors try to withdraw too much of their money at the same time, the bank may not have sufficient reserves on hand to cover those withdrawals. This does occasionally happen. If it should happen to several banks within the same timeframe, it can cause depositors to panic and try to pull *all* their money out, resulting in a cascade of multiple bank failures. This is called a *run on the banks*, and that, too, occasionally happens. A major panic could topple the banking system and have a domino effect on the rest of the economy.

A very recent and potentially important development is that of cryptocurrencies. Bitcoin was the first entirely electronic currency. It is backed by absolutely nothing, not even a fiat! In addition to its electronic speed, convenience, anonymity, and internationality, the good thing about Bitcoin is that the money supply, the number of Bitcoins in electronic circulation, is rigidly regulated. Additional Bitcoins are added at a controlled, slow, and diminishing rate and at a significant cost. The Bitcoin supply is rather inelastic. This is not always the case with some of the other cryptocurrencies that have been introduced as competitors to Bitcoin.

However, as it is with other unbacked currencies, the demand for Bitcoins is entirely determined by psychology! That is, people will value a Bitcoin today based solely upon how much value they think they will be able to exchange it for tomorrow. That can change quickly with the latest news. Consequently, the value of one Bitcoin has gyrated wildly from next to nothing all the way up to the $110,000 range.

If you really enjoy gambling, you might want to exchange some Federal Reserve notes (FRNs) for some Bitcoins. People might not be risking nearly as much money on cryptocurrencies as they are if they had greater confidence in the fiat currencies issued by their governments. But remember, if you suddenly can't find anyone willing to exchange anything of value for your cryptocurrency, it could be worth much less or even zero. It's not even printed on paper. If no one will trade anything of value for your FRN, you might still be able to make some use of it in the bathroom or crumple it up for tinder to start a fire. You'd have truly nothing with a cryptocurrency.

Still, cryptocurrency's features are very attractive: fast, very low-cost, peer-to-peer, anonymous transfers between any two entities with an Internet connection and the security and privacy of encryption with no involvement of a specific third party. Some users take advantage of these features by converting FRNs into a cryptocurrency immediately before a transaction and out of it immediately following each transaction, thereby minimizing exposure to the cryptocurrency by holding it only very briefly.

Perhaps cryptocurrency technology might be used in the future to form a solid representative currency that is guaranteed to be redeemable for some commodity or commodities of intrinsic value. A completely electronic "token" could be used as representative money without the need to ever create, carry, or exchange any physical tokens. Paralysis could result, however, if the Internet should ever go down, or if you are unable for whatever reason to connect to it.

The Currency of the United States

The framers of the US Constitution very much appreciated the importance and benefits of sound money as well as the dangers of having a strong central bank. The Constitution was written in 1787 following considerable currency turmoil in the early days of our republic. As one of the few powers enumerated in Article I, Section 8, Congress was specifically assigned the power and responsibility "to coin Money, regulate the Value thereof, and of foreign Coin, and fix the Standard of Weights and Measures." A relevant part of Article I, Section 10, provides that "no State shall ... coin Money; emit Bills of Credit; make any Thing but gold and silver Coin a Tender in Payment of Debts." The issue of a central bank was debated at the time, some of the Founding Fathers favored one, but the Constitution makes no provision for a central bank.

For approximately 120 years following the ratification of the Constitution, the United States ran fairly smoothly using primarily a hard (commodity) currency based on gold and silver.

Central banks were chartered for stretches of time, but the United States had no central bank for most of this period. However, a series of horrible events spanning a sixty-year period in the twentieth century caused the transformation of the US dollar into a fiat currency and created a peculiar central bank that is not directly controlled by, or even a part of, the government.

Because of the practice of fractional reserve banking, several overextended banks failed in 1907. This precipitated a panic and a run on other banks, some of which then also failed. In what could be termed an overreaction, Congress passed the sweeping Federal Reserve Act in 1913. By it, Congress delegated its constitutionally assigned responsibility for money to an organization to be called the Federal Reserve ("the Fed"). Part of the justification for the Fed was that it would act as a "lender of last resort" to enable banks to ride out runs and thereby forestall panics.

The Fed is indeed a central bank with great powers, but it is *not* part of the federal government. It is a cartel of twelve private banks managed by a seven-member board of governors whose members are appointed by the president and confirmed by the Senate to fourteen-year terms. Other than indirectly through these appointments (or changing the law), the government has no control over what the Fed does.

The Fed is legally required to “report” regularly to Congress, but it is not obligated to take any direction from Congress or the president. All stock of the twelve Fed banks is owned by other private banks called *member banks*. The Fed is not taxed, but whatever it reports as a profit goes to the US Treasury. However, it might be noted that the Fed’s operations have never, in over a hundred years, been subjected to a complete and public audit.

At first, since the dollar was still tied to gold, the Treasury and Fed were somewhat constrained from any huge increase in the money supply. Right after World War II, the dollar was still incredibly strong. It was accepted all over the world as being “as good as gold.” In fact, the dollar was adopted as the reserve currency of the free world. Other currencies were linked to the dollar, and the dollar was, in turn, linked to gold at an exchange rate of $35 per ounce, as agreed to by forty-four nations at the Bretton Woods Conference of 1944.

The final and most serious blow to the dollar came in 1971, when President Nixon "suspended" the redeemability of the dollar, completely severing any ties between the dollar and gold. Dollar redeemability is still "suspended." Today, the dollar is floating around as a pure fiat currency. However, substantially the entire world is using fiat currencies that float relative to each other. The relative "soundness" of each is linked more to the strength and stability of each country's economy than to any inherent characteristic of the currency itself.

Although it is far weaker than it used to be, the dollar is still hanging in as the world's reserve currency, primarily because there so far has not been a significantly stronger currency to challenge it. Some think the Chinese are maneuvering toward having their renminbi replace the dollar as the world's reserve currency. The BRICS (Brazil, Russia, India, China,

South Africa) intergovernmental organization has been accumulating countries and strength, recently adding NATO member Turkey. The BRICS block may eventually move to depose the dollar from its perch as the world's reserve currency. That would be a serious blow to the dollar's strength.

Another of the reasons used to justify the creation of the Fed was that savvy bankers acting as central planners manipulating interest rates and the money supply would be able to better smooth out business cycles, booms, busts, and bubbles. But the Fed's track record has not been good. The Great Depression of 1929 and the early 1930s happened on the Fed's watch, as did the more recent "housing bubble" and ensuing bad recession. There are quite a few somewhat less severe examples that could be cited as well.

Yet another huge justification used for the creation of the Fed was that its independence would remove monetary policy from the control of politicians. (It should be pointed out that you really only need to have a "monetary policy" if you have a fiat currency.) It is surely possible that politicians might have done a worse job, and it is not clear how much influence politicians may have actually had, but the performance of the Fed has been rather dismal.

One of the Fed's most important duties is to keep the value of the dollar constant, avoiding either inflation or deflation. There have been three decades under the Fed in which the dollar lost more than 40% of its value during the ten-year period and one decade when it actually gained 23% (deflation). Overall, under the Fed, the dollar has lost about 97% of its purchasing power! That is, the dollar in 2025 is worth less than three cents of the 1913 dollar. The Fed's currently stated objective is to achieve and maintain a 2% per year inflation rate, not zero.

In recent decades, politicians, with the Fed's complicity, have been digging the United States into a very deep hole. In an attempt to "buy votes" to improve their chances of being reelected, politicians like to hand out benefits that cost money — a lot of money. Thus, they have become incorrigibly addicted to spending. These politicians are aided by leftists who do not understand a free market economy and some actively favor a command economy. Federal spending is growing and approaching the $5 trillion per year range. Government is no longer the small percentage of "overhead" that it used to be and has become quite significant compared to the entire output of the economy — the *gross domestic product* (GDP) — which was approximately $29 trillion in 2024.

A balanced budget would require politicians to reduce spending or raise taxes to pay for their handouts. However, increasing taxes would damage their electability. Governments at all levels are already confiscating a huge percentage—an average of nearly one-third—of the private sector's earnings. When this much "blood" is drained from the body and spent inefficiently, the economy struggles to sustain even a slow rate of growth (1% to 3% per year).

Things got totally out of control a few years back when the politicians figured out that they could avoid the immediate pain of imposing higher taxes by just borrowing money and postponing the pain to the future. By the end of 2024, they had run up more than $36 trillion in debt at the federal level. That was larger than the GDP;

indeed, it was close to 125% of the GDP. That's a whole bunch of future pain. It is terribly wrong to inflict such pain on future generations, especially since they have no say in the matter.

In addition, they have legislated large "entitlement" programs that have become actuarially unsound. The unfunded liabilities for these programs are not included in the $36 trillion debt figure and are many times larger. Considerable additional debt resides at the state and local government levels. An increasing number of cities have gone belly-up, and some states (e.g., Illinois and California) are in danger of bankruptcy.

While the politicians have been spending and the Treasury borrowing, the Treasury and Fed have been expanding the money supply at an unprecedented rate. Inflationary pressures are running high. Excessive relief spending related to the 2021–2022 COVID pandemic and "climate change" programs pushed inflation up to more than 9%. Of course, it's nice to be able to pay off debt (Treasury bonds) with dollars that are worth less, but inflation necessarily pushes up interest rates. Interest on the national debt was $659 billion in 2023.

Interest has become such a large line item in the federal budget that it is forcing either cuts in other spending or even more borrowing. The government is near the danger point of spiraling into bankruptcy. The credit rating agencies have started reducing the United States' credit rating. US Treasury bonds have always been considered the safest of places to stash money. That has allowed the United States to borrow at very low interest rates, but that obviously is changing, and investors are going to insist upon higher interest payments to offset the increasing risk. That also will force interest on the national debt upwards. Said interest could soon exceed a trillion dollars per year.

The politicians have spent the country into a very difficult and dangerous financial position. Will they stop? Not likely. They appear to be more concerned with staying in power than they are about the country's welfare. It seems that they will continue kicking the can down the road, hoping that serious problems can be forestalled until they are out of office or ready to retire. Very serious federal austerity or a large devaluation of our currency or both can't be very far down the road. The economy would have to show sustained growth at an unrealistically high rate in order to "grow our way out of" this jam.

With careful, resolute, and even-handed management, it *might* be possible to pull back from the brink and gradually climb or grow our way out of the hole. However, regardless of how it is done, there would unavoidably be very noticeable pain involved. Based on our dismal history, there is no reason to anticipate careful, resolute, and even-handed management.

Barring a miracle (like a majority of intelligent, honest, responsible politicians), it appears that the end of our fiat currency is now coming into view in the not-too-distant future. Exactly when a collapse may come and what will trigger it is impossible to predict accurately. This is especially so now that ours is one of many unstable fiat currencies floating around relative to each other; one can draw at least temporary strength from the relative weakness of others. But don't look down.

3. The Path to Prosperity

The very first requirement for prosperity is a properly operating free market economic system. Many think the US already has a free market economy, but they would be only somewhat correct. The US economy has drifted farther and farther toward a command economy as governments have become more and more intrusive with regulations, tax and spend programs, and other manipulations. To everyone's detriment, all such things throw sand in the gears and reduce the rate at which the economy can create wealth. A free market economic system cannot operate at its best (highest rate of wealth creation) if there is any force involved. Everything in a pure free market economy must be the result of voluntary interactions and transactions among free people pursuing their rational self-interests.

The laws of economics have, of course, always existed, but human understanding of them began with the science of economics at about the time of the American Revolution. Much more widespread economic "literacy" surely would be helpful, especially in Congress. Markets are complex, with billions of interacting feedback loops at many levels that maintain equilibrium. Economic interactions, causes, and effects are hard to fully understand and can often be counterintuitive. The free market may not be completely without problems, but it surely is far better than anything else that has been tried or conceived.

The greatest threat to a free market economy is politicians attempting to manipulate the economy through the use of government force. Sometimes, this may even be a well-intentioned attempt to "fix" some sort of real or perceived "problem." Other times, it is just a payoff to a crony or special interest group. Common examples are

- generally heavy taxation that drains wealth from the economy to support constitutionally unauthorized government activities, to be spent inefficiently, or to fund waste, fraud, and abuse;

- targeted punitive taxation intended to reduce the demand for some good or service (e.g., “vice taxes” on alcohol, tobacco, and marijuana);

- crazily complex tax laws that require the huge wasted overhead of an entire industry of accountants, tax preparers, and advisers to help people comply with tax laws;

- subsidization aimed at lowering the (apparent) cost, increasing the supply, and spurring the purchase of some good or service (e.g., solar cells and battery electric vehicles);

- guarantees, where taxpayers are put on the hook to guarantee loans or deals;

- forcing or prohibiting the use of some good or service (e.g., ethanol in gasoline);

- attempting to force minimum or maximum prices for goods and services (e.g., minimum wage laws or price controls);

- bogus licensing requirements intended to shield established members of an industry (who hire good lobbyists and fund them well) from new competition; and

- confiscation of wealth earned by one individual and either giving it to another individual who did not earn it, or spending it in accordance with politicians' priorities.

The only highly efficient spending is when you spend your own wealth on things that you want or need. The lowest efficiency is 536 politicians spending your money on themselves, their cronies, or for things they *think* citizens should want or need.

To the extent that the above distortions occur, we do not have a free market. All such actions have both some consequences that are seen and many that are unseen. Overall, *the result is to misallocate resources and reduce the rate of wealth creation*, thus penalizing everyone either directly or indirectly. All too often, unforeseen consequences even make the targeted problem itself worse instead of better.

The US economy is so distorted by so many such actions that it struggles to achieve 1% to 4% per year growth in "good" years when it could and should be humming along at 7% to 9% per year growth, possibly more. That's a whole bunch of wealth that's not being created and not raising everyone's standard of living. The United States needs to move strongly away from the command economy end of the spectrum and back toward the free market end.

How and why has this been allowed to happen? The root cause is widespread and amazingly profound economic illiteracy. Very few people comprehend how a free market economy works. Even those who advocate for the free market economic system seldom understand it well enough to explain it and defend it effectively. This should not be surprising as the schools do not teach microeconomics well, if at all. The situation is so bad that there is a dearth of teachers capable of teaching it. No student should graduate from high school without a good understanding of the free market economic system.

What can you do about it if you are economically illiterate? The best cure would be to take a good microeconomics 101 course. That may not be a practical possibility for many, but there is a reasonable stopgap alternative. Several rather effective and short books are available that do a fine job of providing a basic understanding of how a free market economy works. *Economics in One Easy Lesson* by Henry Hazlitt is a classic. *How to Think about the Economy* by Per L. Bylund is another. Perhaps the shortest and easiest to read is the new one, *The Savior of the World – Comprehending the Free Market Economic System* that is listed at the end of the About the Author section.

One of the things you will learn is that the proper operation of a free market economy requires sound money. As previously discussed, we do not have sound money in the US, and that is more or less true for other countries as well.

Sound Money

If we could "design" our money from the ground up, what choices should we make?

As we have seen, any truly sound money *must* either have an intrinsic value itself (commodity money) or be representative money that is *guaranteed* to be redeemable for something of value upon demand. The latter is certainly the preferred choice in our high-tech world, in which transactions are increasingly handled by adjusting numbers in computers rather than physically transferring pieces of paper or metal.

We reject fiat money simply because, for the reasons discussed, it cannot be depended upon to perform the three functions of money well over long periods of time. Its stability is poor, and its collapse almost invariably is highly disruptive.

Commodity money and representative money arose spontaneously and independently of any government. It would be preferable to maintain independence from any political entity so that our new money could be used within any region or the entire world, just as gold coins maintain substantially the same value (relative to other commodities) anywhere. This last objective is extremely difficult to achieve in today's world.

Certainly, there would be no attempt to prohibit the use of any competing forms of money. Since sound money is always preferred to unsound money, our new money should be preferred if we've designed it correctly. If not, oh well, somebody else did a better job and therefore should prevail. Free competition is always a good thing. Finally, sound money cannot be used as a tool to facilitate extreme financial irresponsibility by governments—for example, paying back borrowed funds with money that is worth less than that borrowed.

We come now to the question of what should back our currency. For what should holders of the currency be guaranteed to be able to exchange it upon demand? It would probably not be a horrible mistake to choose gold. Gold has been used successfully over long periods of time. It seems likely that this will continue to be the case in the future—but, of course, there is no guarantee of that. Perhaps gold will be supplanted by something else in its industrial and cosmetic uses so that its demand decreases. Or maybe new uses for gold might be found that increase the demand for it. Or perhaps some new way of mining, refining, or creating gold will be invented that drastically increases its supply. Any of those things might cause the value of gold relative to other things to change significantly. Note that such dramatic changes can and do occasionally occur. A prime example is diamonds. Advancing technology has enabled the manufacture of diamonds that are both higher in quality and significantly lower in cost that those naturally occurring.

Although gold would be far better than the current situation of no backing, perhaps a way can be devised to improve upon gold as a backing for currency. The choice of the best thing to back our currency turns out to be more complex than one might initially think. Unfortunately, there is no absolute scale of value. All commodities are valued relative to each other, and worse, the relative valuations change over time, sometimes dramatically. A great example of such dramatic change can be found in anything electronic. Advancing technology has made all things electronic cost less in terms of the dollar, even in the face of inflation that makes the dollar itself worth less; at the same time, the functionality, reliability, and other characteristics of electronic products have all improved greatly. So, what really does it mean to keep the value of the dollar "constant"? To what can one anchor the value of a representative currency in this vast sea of shifting values with no land ever in sight?

Economics is all about satisfying the wants of humans. Rather than tie our new currency to one commodity, it would seem better to tie it to something of great and lasting significance to humans. There are many ways this could be done, but it's hard to think of anything of more universal and fundamental human significance than the "cost of living." Indexes have been devised which are intended to measure the cost of living. We use them to measure inflation, so the concept of the cost of living is nothing new.

Suppose you are a descendant of Rip Van Winkle and you like to take long naps. You are planning a nice twenty-five-year nap. You realize that many things will change unpredictably over that amount of time. You know that you will not have a job when you awake and that you may have to live for a while without one. You may have a fair amount to learn in order to get back up to speed, nail down a job, and become self-supporting again. This is bound to take some time. To prepare responsibly, you stash enough cash under your mattress to support yourself in a reasonable (say, middle-class) manner for a year.

When you awake twenty-five years later, it seems entirely reasonable to expect that your stashed cash will indeed support you in a then-equivalent middle-class style for a year. You certainly should not be rudely surprised to find that your cash now will support you for only four months!

Of course, a lot of things may have changed while you slept. It might be that buggy whips were part of your cost of living when you went to bed, but when you wake up, buggy whips are no longer part of your cost of living, but gasoline is. What should not change, though, is the cost of living. If you can support yourself with a middle-class existence for $50,000 per year today, you should be able to support yourself equivalently for a year for $50,000 tomorrow or twenty-five years later or a hundred years later. Money can do a pretty good job of acting as a store of value if it is measured in terms of some well-chosen commodity. But it could do an even better job of storing value if that value is of direct, fundamental, and more universal value to humans. How might this be accomplished?

A carefully designed and maintained cost-of-living index would have to be at the core. It should be composed of a large number of goods and services, each widely and frequently traded, with weighting factors so as to always accurately represent and total up to the median cost of living at any given time. All prices are, say, fifty-two-week moving averages updated weekly, so there is a great deal of stability and no seasonality. No single component can have more than a minuscule impact upon the total. As the impact of things like buggy whips upon the median cost of living fades, their weighting factors are slowly reduced, while the weighting factors for things with growing impacts (gasoline) are increased to reflect their growing significance.

It obviously is of the utmost importance that the index be honestly and impartially maintained by an independent entity immune to any political or economic influences. Note that the Consumer Price Index (CPI) maintained by the US government has been modified several times to show lower rates of inflation. For example, food and fuel have been removed as components of the CPI ostensibly because of their "volatility." But who believes food and fuel are not significant to the cost of living? One of the reasons for such manipulations is that cost-of-living adjustments based on the CPI are reduced, somewhat easing budgetary problems like the growth of Social Security payments. It should be possible to fairly rigidly define the procedure for determining the cost of living in such a way as to minimize the opportunity for nefarious manipulation.

The cost of living can be expected to remain quite constant naturally. It is not appreciably affected by the normal short-term fluctuations in the prices of its many components. It could be expected to change slowly over the long term as affected by, say, technology tending to reduce costs and/or the gradual phasing in and out of components (gasoline instead of buggy whips, etc.) or even an increasing standard of living.

Suppose that the cost of living when our new index is initiated is $50,000. This then becomes the reference cost of living. Each time the cost of living is updated, it is divided into the reference cost of living to obtain an *adjustment factor*. If the cost of living always stays $50,000 (as is the goal), the adjustment factor is always 1.00000. However, suppose in some future week the cost of living computes to $50,100.00. The adjustment factor then becomes 0.99800. Of course, if the cost of living starts to drift down below $50,000, the adjustment factor will be greater than 1.0000. A cost-of-living computation of $49,900.00 results in an adjustment factor of 1.00200. The trick now is to implement a negative feedback loop that will adjust the value of the dollar so that the adjustment factor stays very close to 1.00000 and therefore always keeps the cost of living very near $50,000.

With a fiat currency, such a feedback loop has to be created by linking the money supply to the adjustment factor. If/when the adjustment factor drops below 1.00000 (inflation), the US Treasury must judiciously decrease the money supply. This tends to increase the value of the dollar and cause prices to generally decline. In the opposite case, where the adjustment factor goes above 1.00000 (deflation), the money supply must be increased, thereby decreasing the value of the dollar and causing a general increase in prices back to a $50,000 cost of living. The volatility of fiat currencies (previously discussed) combined with hard-to-predict time delays between changes in the money supply and the resultant price changes make this feedback loop somewhat tricky but certainly better than no control.

A hard currency, guaranteed to always be redeemable for something of intrinsic value, is fundamentally much less volatile and more stable. The dollar itself could be intrinsically worthless paper, coins, or a cryptocurrency. The feedback loop established above could be stabilized and the fiat currency converted to a representative currency by guaranteeing its redeemability. But how could that be done, and for what exactly would it be redeemable?

Again utilizing the adjustment factor, the dollar could be made redeemable for anything that is convenient. If we wish to redeem the dollar for gold, this can be done by multiplying the current spot price for gold by the adjustment factor. Similarly, the dollar could be redeemed for silver at a rate determined simply by multiplying silver's current spot price by the adjustment factor. Indeed, the dollar could be redeemed in *any* convenient commodity that a depository institution and its customers might agree to use; just multiply the current market price of the commodity by the adjustment factor to obtain the redemption rate. In this manner, the dollar could be solidly anchored to the cost of living.

Note that under the system just described, fluctuations in the price of gold, silver, or any commodity are not at all disruptive, as the dollar is now decoupled from any particular commodity. The dollar is now a solid representative currency that is guaranteed to be redeemable but not necessarily for a fixed amount of any specific commodity. One cannot say that the dollar represents gold, silver, barley, or any commodity, although it could indeed be redeemed for any of them. So, what exactly is it that the dollar represents? Using the numbers from the above examples, the dollar always represents slightly more than ten minutes of middle-class living.

The guarantee of redeemability is important, of course, but there is no reason to think that it would be much used. As long as the value of the dollar remains constant, there is no reason to redeem it, especially since there will need to be a small (say, 1%) fee for the redemption transaction to cover costs. If the dollar deflates (becomes worth more and the adjustment factor rises above 1.00000), the redemption commodity could be purchased for less on the open market. It is only in the case of inflation (the dollar loses value, is worth less, and the correction factor falls below 1.00000) that anyone would be motivated to redeem it. That is why the government is very strongly incentivized to do the best possible job of keeping the value of the dollar constant.

Conclusions

It should be possible to gain the manifold advantages of a hard representative currency without the potential disadvantage of tying it to some specific commodity. Instead, its flexibly redeemable value could be locked to follow any gradual long-term shifts in what is probably most important to humans: their cost of living. Cost-of-living adjustments would never be needed. The ability to plan for the future would be simplified and improved. Interest rates likely would be more stable. An overall approach to accomplishing this has been outlined.

A hard currency is its own monetary policy. There is no need for central planning or manipulation. A central bank is not necessary, and the potential problems of a central bank can be avoided.

Interest rates (the rental price for money) should be set by normal free market forces from competition among many borrowers and many lenders, just as all other prices should be determined by market supply and demand. Operating without the use of force, the myriads of corrective feedback loops of a voluntary free market automatically do the best job of maintaining balance and efficiently allocating resources. Arbitrary manipulation of anything is undesirable and almost inevitably destabilizing, especially when attempted in combination with the inherent instability of a fiat currency

Before concluding this topic, it may be interesting to contemplate for just a moment the nature of money. It is purely human. Outside of that limited realm, money makes absolutely no sense and has no use or purpose at all. The basic idea of money and its function is entirely a construct of the human intellect. It, and indeed even the economies to which money is essential, are the product of our specie's (so far) unique ability for rational thought. Think about it.

About the Author

Although Roy Minet's major in college was physics, he accepted a particularly interesting job offer in engineering with a large multi-national corporation as his first employment. That led to positions in sales, marketing, then marketing management, and finally management of a strategic business planning department, all for the same corporation.

Moving into small business, he bought and operated a master beer distributorship for 12 years before selling it. While distributing (and perhaps drinking) beer, he founded Intelligent Computer Systems, Inc., which pioneered comprehensive, integrated, real-time business software and installed turnkey computer systems for distribution businesses nationwide. After 22 years, ICS was sold to the 3M Corporation.

Mr. Minet is now retired and pursuing a backlog of personal projects—most notably, improving all aspects of elections. Work done in 2009 produced the Precinct-Preserving Splitline (PPS) geometric procedure—an elegant cure for gerrymandering. In 2020, he proposed the Approve/Approve/Disapprove Voting (AADV) method as the best replacement for the plurality method—finally resolving the 240-year-long voting methods debate. The Election Manager system, comprehensive software to run all aspects of elections, was developed in

2011, then revised in 2021 to include the AADV method.

Mr. Minet also has taught economics in 11th and 12th grades with the Junior Achievement program. Approximately 40 of his op-ed columns have been published. He was the Libertarian Party's candidate for Pennsylvania Auditor General in 2016.

Website: https://royminet.org/

Other books by Roy A. Minet

The Savior of the World — Comprehending the Free Market Economic System

Available here: https://books2read.com/TheSaviorOfTheWorldByRoyMinet

Elections Are Broken — How to Fix Them

Available here: https://books2read.com/ElectionsAreBrokenByRoyMinet

Everything Rational thinking and the human race from its beginning to its end.

Available here:
https://books2read.com/EverythingByRoyMinet

www.ingramcontent.com/pod-product-compliance
Lightning Source LLC
LaVergne TN
LVHW022321200926
848481LV00004B/1385

* 9 7 9 8 2 3 1 4 3 3 4 0 7 *

Do **you** really understand money? Should you buy some Bitcoin How about gold? Silver? What causes inflation? What are th three functions that money needs to perform well? What are th three different kinds of money, and which kind is cryptocurrency

Everyone deals with money on a daily basis. Few give it mucl thought. But if you're a bit fuzzy about the answers to any of th above questions, it could be hazardous to your wealth. Mone causes many problems, some quite disruptive. Sound money i crucial to the proper functioning of a free market economy.

This short, easy-to-read book clearly explains. It provides th knowledge to answer the above questions and many more. As bonus, the ultimate sound currency will be designed.

Other Books by Roy A. Minet

The Savior of the World -- Comprehending the Fre Market Economic System

Elections Are Broken — How to Fix Them

Everything **The human race from its beginning to it end.**

ISBN 979-8-231-43340-7

90000

9 798231 433407